TULSA CITY-COUNTY LIBRARY

FOR REFERENCE

MAY 14 2011

Cram101 Textbook Outlines to accompany:

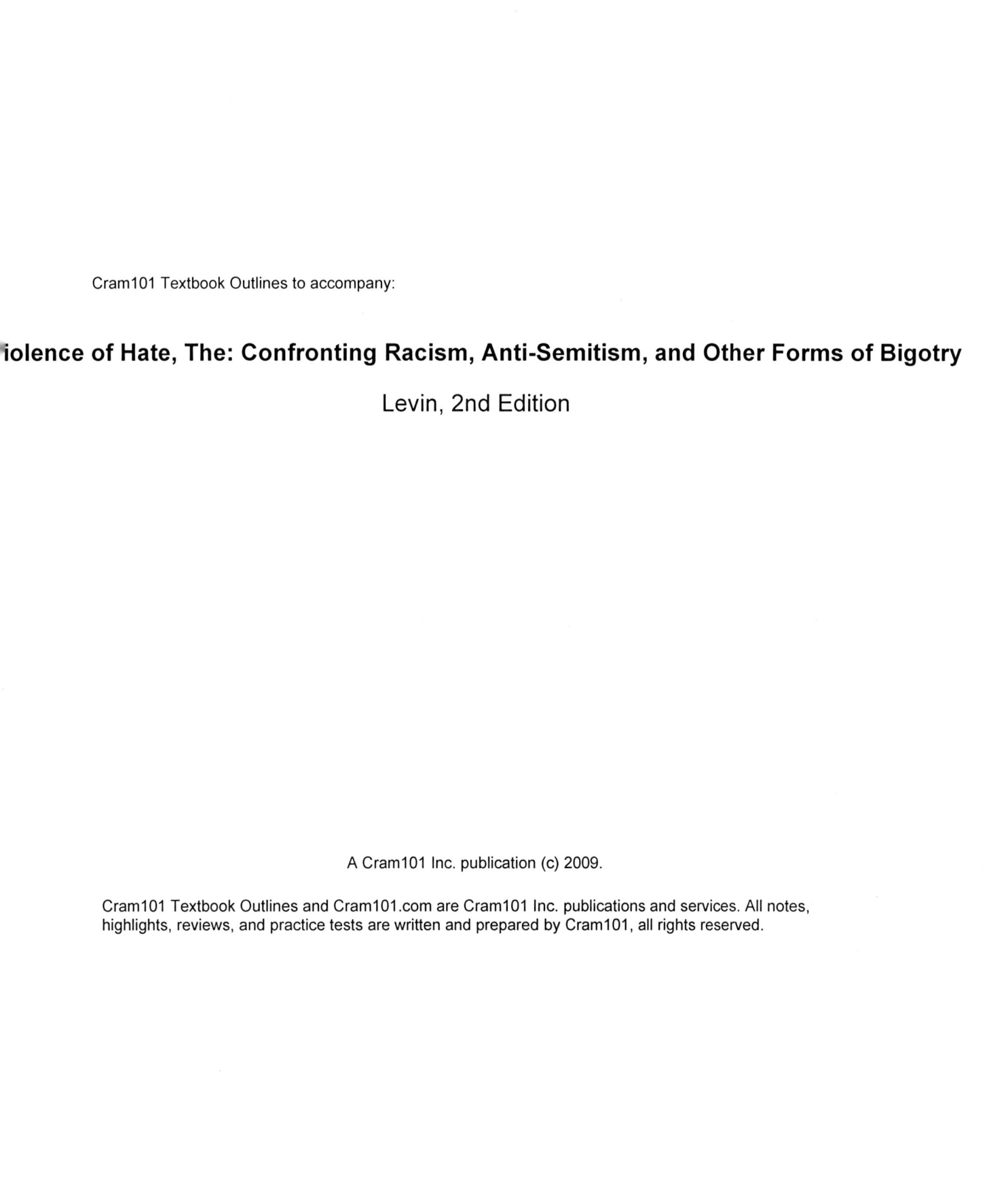

Violence of Hate, The: Confronting Racism, Anti-Semitism, and Other Forms of Bigotry

Levin, 2nd Edition

A Cram101 Inc. publication (c) 2009.

Cram101 Textbook Outlines and Cram101.com are Cram101 Inc. publications and services. All notes, highlights, reviews, and practice tests are written and prepared by Cram101, all rights reserved.

PRACTICE EXAMS.

Get all of the self-teaching practice exams for each chapter of this textbook at **www.Cram101.com** and ace the tests. Here is an example:

Chapter 1

Violence of Hate, The: Confronting Racism, Anti-Semitism, and Other Forms of Bigotry
Levin, 2nd Edition,
All Material Written and Prepared by Cram101

I WANT A BETTER GRADE. Items 1 - 50 of 100.

1. _____ is a state in the Mid-Atlantic and Northeastern regions of the United States of America. With 62 counties, it is the country's third most populous state. It is bordered by Vermont, Massachusetts, Connecticut, New Jersey, and Pennsylvania, and shares a water border with Rhode Island as well as an international border with the Canadian provinces of Quebec and Ontario. Its five largest cities are _____ City, Buffalo, Rochester, Yonkers, and Syracuse.

   ○ New York ○ New Jersey
   ○ New Mexico ○ New York City

2. _____ two key demographic features are its population density and cultural diversity. It is exceptionally diverse. Throughout its history the city has been a major point of entry for immigrants; the term "melting pot" was first coined to describe densely populated immigrant neighborhoods on the Lower East Side. Violent crime in _____ has decreased 75% in the last twelve years and the murder rate.

   ○ New York City ○ New Jersey
   ○ New Mexico ○ New York

3. _____ is an emotion of intense revulsion, distaste, enmity, or antipathy for a person, thing, or phenomenon, generally attributed to a desire to avoid, restrict, remove, or destroy the hated object. _____ can be based on fear of an object or past negative consequences of dealing with that object.

   ○ Hatred ○ Habeas corpus
   ○ Habitat ○ Hacienda system

You get a 50% discount for the online exams. Go to **Cram101.com**, click Sign Up at the top of the screen, and enter DK73DW4491 in the promo code box on the registration screen. Access to Cram101.com is $4.95 per month, cancel at any time.

With Cram101.com online, you also have access to extensive reference material.

You will nail those essays and papers. Here is an example from a Cram101 Biology text:

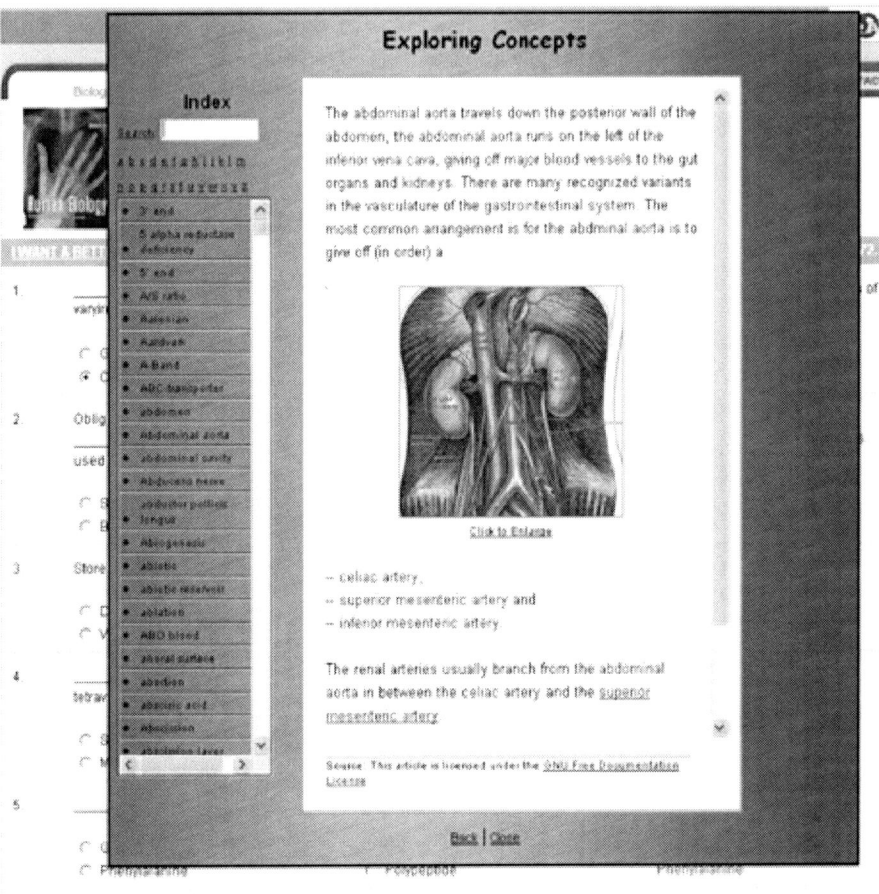

Visit **www.Cram101.com**, click Sign Up at the top of the screen, and enter DK73DW4491 in the promo code box on the registration screen. Access to www.Cram101.com is normally $9.95 per month, but because you have purchased this book, your access fee is only $4.95 per month, cancel at any time. Sign up and stop highlighting textbooks forever.

Learning System

Cram101 Textbook Outlines is a learning system. The notes in this book are the highlights of your textbook, you will never have to highlight a book again.

How to use this book. Take this book to class, it is your notebook for the lecture. The notes and highlights on the left hand side of the pages follow the outline and order of the textbook. All you have to do is follow along while your instructor presents the lecture. Circle the items emphasized in class and add other important information on the right side. With Cram101 Textbook Outlines you'll spend less time writing and more time listening. Learning becomes more efficient.

Cram101.com Online

Increase your studying efficiency by using Cram101.com's practice tests and online reference material. It is the perfect complement to Cram101 Textbook Outlines. Use self-teaching matching tests or simulate in-class testing with comprehensive multiple choice tests, or simply use Cram's true and false tests for quick review. Cram101.com even allows you to enter your in-class notes for an integrated studying format combining the textbook notes with your class notes.

Visit **www.Cram101.com**, click Sign Up at the top of the screen, and enter **DK73DW4491** in the promo code box on the registration screen. Access to www.Cram101.com is normally $9.95, but because you have purchased this book, your access fee is only $4.95. Sign up and stop highlighting textbooks forever.

Copyright © 2009 by Cram101, Inc. All rights reserved. "Cram101"® and "Never Highlight a Book Again!"® are registered trademarks of Cram101, Inc. ISBN(s): 1-4288-6356-7, 9781428863569 .

Violence of Hate, The: Confronting Racism, Anti-Semitism, and Other Forms of Bigotry
Levin, 2nd

CONTENTS

1. Perspectives on Hate and Violence 2
2. A Typology of Hate 20
3. The Benefits of Bigotry 32
4. The Production of Rebels, Deviants, and Other Decent People 40

Chapter 1. Perspectives on Hate and Violence

New York	New York is a state in the Mid-Atlantic and Northeastern regions of the United States of America. With 62 counties, it is the country's third most populous state. It is bordered by Vermont, Massachusetts, Connecticut, New Jersey, and Pennsylvania, and shares a water border with Rhode Island as well as an international border with the Canadian provinces of Quebec and Ontario. Its five largest cities are New York City, Buffalo, Rochester, Yonkers, and Syracuse.
New York City	New York City two key demographic features are its population density and cultural diversity. It is exceptionally diverse. Throughout its history the city has been a major point of entry for immigrants; the term "melting pot" was first coined to describe densely populated immigrant neighborhoods on the Lower East Side. Violent crime in New York city has decreased 75% in the last twelve years and the murder rate.
Hatred	Hatred is an emotion of intense revulsion, distaste, enmity, or antipathy for a person, thing, or phenomenon, generally attributed to a desire to avoid, restrict, remove, or destroy the hated object. Hatred can be based on fear of an object or past negative consequences of dealing with that object.
Murder	Murder is the unlawful, premeditated killing of a human being by another. The penalty for murder is usually either life imprisonment, or in jurisdictions with capital punishment, the death penalty.
Prejudice	Prejudice is, as the name implies, the process of "pre-judging" something. It implies coming to a judgment on a subject before learning where the preponderance of evidence actually lies, or forming a judgment without direct experience.
Gordon W. Allport	Gordon W. Allport was an American psychologist. He rejected both a psychoanalytic approach to personality, which he thought often went too deep, and a behavioral approach, which he thought often did not go deep enough. He was one of the first researchers to draw a distinction between Motive and Drive. He suggested that a drive formed as a reaction to a motive may out-grow the motive as a reason.
Bias	A bias is a prejudice in a general or specific sense, usually in the sense for having a preference to one particular point of view or ideological perspective.
Authoritarianism	Authoritarianism describes a form of government characterized by strict obedience to the authority of the state, which often maintains and enforces social control through the use of oppressive measures. The term may also be used to describe the personality or management style of an individual or organization which seeks to dominate those within its sphere of influence and has little regard for building consensus.
Authoritarian personality	A set of distinctive personality traits, including conformity, intolerance, and an inability to accept ambiguity, is referred to as an authoritarian personality.
Bigotry	A bigot is a person who is intolerant of opinions, lifestyles, or identities differing from his or her own, and bigotry is the corresponding state of mind. Forms of bigotry may have a related ideology or world views.
Groups	In sociology, a group can be defined as two or more humans that interact with one another, accept expectations and obligations as members of the group, and share a common identity. By this definition, society can be viewed as a large group, though most social groups are considerably smaller.
Individualism	Individualism is a term used to describe a moral, political, or social outlook that stresses human independence and the importance of self-reliance and liberty. They promote the exercise of their goals and desires. They oppose most external interference with their choices - whether by society, the state, or any other group or institution.
Personality	In psychology, personality is a description of consistent emotional, thought, and behavior patterns in a person. The several theoretical perspectives on personality involve different ideas about the relationship between personality and other psychological constructs as well as different ideas about

Chapter 1. Perspectives on Hate and Violence

	the way personality doesn't develop.
Christian	A Christian is a person who adheres to Christianity, a monotheistic religion centered on the life and teachings of Jesus Christ as presented in the New Testament and interpreted by Christians to have been prophesied in the Hebrew Bible/Old Testament.
Civil rights	Civil rights are the protections and privileges of personal liberty given to all citizens by law. Civil rights are rights that are bestowed by nations on those within their territorial boundaries.
Civil rights movement	Historically, the civil rights movement was a concentrated period of time around the world of approximately one generation (1954-1980) wherein there was much worldwide civil unrest and popular rebellion.
Identity	Identity is an umbrella term used throughout the social sciences to describe an individual's comprehension of him or herself as a discrete, separate entity.
Social science	The social science is a group of academic disciplines that study human aspects of the world. They diverge from the arts and humanities in that the social science tends to emphasize the use of the scientific method in the study of humanity, including quantitative and qualitative methods. The social science, in studying subjective, inter-subjective and objective or structural aspects of society, were traditionally referred to as soft sciences.
Concept	As the term is used in mainstream cognitive science and philosophy of mind, a concept is an abstract idea or a mental symbol, typically associated with a corresponding representation in and language or symbology.
Racism	Racism, by its simplest definition, is discrimination based on race. People with racist beliefs might hate certain groups of people according to their race, or in the case of institutional racism, certain racial groups may be denied rights or benefits. Racism typically starts with the assumption that there are taxonomic differences between different groups of people. According to the United Nations conventions, there is no distinction between the term racial discrimination and ethnic discrimination.
Apartheid	Apartheid was a system of racial segregation in South Africa. The rules of Apartheid dictated that people be legally classified into racial groups -- the main ones were Black, White, Coloured and Indian -- and separated from one another on the basis of legal classification and unequal rights.
Violence	Violence is, on the one hand, acts of aggression and abuse that cause' or intend to cause injury to person or persons. Central to this concept of violence is the presence of the definite intention to cause significant injury, damage and harm.
Negro	Negro is a term referring to people of Black African ancestry. Prior to the shift in the lexicon of American and worldwide classification of race and ethnicity in the late 1960s, the appellation was accepted as a normal neutral formal term both by those of Black African descent as well as non-African blacks.
Racial identity	Racial identity refers to identification with a particular racial category ; distinct from ethnic identity .
Social construction	A social construction is an institutionalized entity or artifact in a social system 'invented' or 'constructed' by participants in a particular culture or society that exists solely because people agree to behave as if it exists, or agree to follow certain conventional rules.
Census	A census is the process of obtaining information about every member of a population. It can be contrasted with sampling in which information is only obtained from a subset of a population. As such it is a method used for accumulating statistical data, and it is also vital to democracy.
Marriage	A marriage is an interpersonal relationship with governmental, social, or religious recognition, usually intimate and sexual, and often created as a contract. The most frequently occurring form of marriage unites a man and a woman as husband and wife. Other forms of marriage also exist; for

Chapter 1. Perspectives on Hate and Violence

Chapter 1. Perspectives on Hate and Violence

	example, polygamy, in which a person takes more than one spouse, is common in many societies
Tiger Woods	Tiger Woods whose achievements to date rank him among the most successful golfers of all time. Currently the World No. 1, Woods was the highest-paid professional athlete in 2007, having earned an estimated $122 million from winnings and endorsements. According to Golf Digest, Woods made $769,440,709 from 1996 to 2007, and the magazine predicts that by 2010, Woods will become the world's first athlete to pass one billion dollars in earnings.
Interracial	The word interracial may be used in reference to the mixing of people of different races that results from racial integration or desegregation.
Stereotype	A stereotype is a simplified and/or standardized conception or image with specific meaning, often held in common by one group of people about another group. A stereotype can be a conventional and oversimplified conception, opinion, or image, based on the assumption that there are attributes that members of the other group hold in common. Stereotypes may be positive or negative in tone. They are typically generalizations based on minimal or limited knowledge about a group to which the person doing the stereotyping does not belong. Persons may be grouped based on race, ethnicity, religion, sexual orientation, or any number of other categories.
Dehumanization	Dehumanization is a process by which members of a group of people assert the "inferiority" of another group through subtle or overt acts or statements. Dehumanization may be directed by an organization or may be the composite of individual sentiments and actions, as with some types of de facto racism.
Immigration	Although human migration has existed for hundreds of thousands of years, immigration in the modern sense refers to movement of people from one nation-state to another, where they are not citizens.
Northern Ireland	Northern Ireland has been for many years the site of a violent and bitter ethno-political conflict between those claiming to represent Nationalists, who are predominantly Catholic, and those claiming to represent Unionists, who are predominantly Protestant. In general, Nationalists want Northern Ireland to be unified with the Republic of Ireland, and Unionists want it to remain part of the United Kingdom. Unionists are in the majority in Northern Ireland, though Nationalists represent a significant minority.
Religion	A religion is a set of common beliefs and practices generally held by a group of people, often codified as prayer, ritual, and religious law. Religion also encompasses ancestral or cultural traditions, writings, history, and mythology, as well as personal faith and mystic experience.
Slavery	Slavery refers to an extreme form of stratification in which some people are owned by others.
Prison	A prison is a place in which individuals are physically confined or interned, and usually deprived of a range of personal freedoms. Prisons are conventionally institutions which form part of the criminal justice system of a country, such that incarceration is a legal penalty that may be imposed by the state for the commission of a crime.
Crime	A normative definition views crime as deviant behavior that violates prevailing norms, specifically, cultural standards prescribing how humans ought to behave.
Hate crimes	Hate crimes occur when a perpetrator targets a victim because of his or her membership in a certain social group, usually defined by race, religion, sexual orientation, disability, ethnicity, nationality, age, gender, gender identity, or political affiliation. Hate crimes differ from conventional crime because they are not directed simply at an individual, but are meant to cause fear and intimidation in an entire group or class of people.
Aryan	Aryan is an English language word derived from Sanskrit and Avestan ârya- meaning "noble". It is widely held to have been used as an ethnic self-designation of the Proto-Indo-Iranians. Since, in the 19th century, the Indo-Iranians were the most ancient known speakers of Indo-European languages, the word Aryan was adopted to refer not only to the Indo-Iranian people, but also to Indo-European speakers as a whole.

Chapter 1. Perspectives on Hate and Violence

Aryan Nation	The Aryan Nation is a White Nationalist, Neo-Nazi organization which was founded by Richard Girnt Butler as an arm of the Christian Identity group Church of Jesus Christ-Christian. The group has been called a "terrorist threat" by the FBI, and the RAND Corporation has called it the "first truly nationwide terrorist network." Its origin lies in the teachings of Wesley Swift, a significant figure in the early Christian Identity movement.
Aryan Nations	Aryan Nations is an international white supremacist, Neo-Nazi organization. It was founded in the 1970s by Richard Girnt Butler as an arm of the Christian Identity group Church of Jesus Christ-Christian.
Integration	Social integration is a term used in sociology and several other social sciences. The term indicates different meanings depending on the context. In general, it connotes the process of combining a group of persons like minority groups, ethnic minorities, refugees, underprivileged sections of the society, to integrate into the mainstream of the society, and thus to avail of the opportunities, rights and services available to the members of the mainstream of the society. It is important to note that within the field of sociology social integration usually goes hand in hand with social solidarity and anomie.
Sikh	Sikh is the title and name given to an adherent of Sikhism. The evolution of it began with the emergence of Guru Nanak as a religious leader and a social reformer during the fifteenth century in Punjab. It established a nation, under Ranjit Singh, in the nineteenth century in which they were preeminent. They were known for their military prowess, administrative capabilties, economic productivity and their adaptability to modern western technology and administration.
Xenophobia	Xenophobia is a fear or contempt of foreigners or strangers. The term is typically used to describe fear or dislike of foreigners or in general of people different from one's self.
Decline	Decline is a change over time from previously efficient to inefficient organizational functioning, from previously rational to non-rational organizational and individual decision-making, from previously law-abiding to law violating organizational and individual behavior, from previously virtuous to iniquitous individual moral behavior.
Minority	A minority is a sociological group that does not constitute a politically dominant plurality of the total population of a given society. A sociological minority is not necessarily a numerical minority it may include any group that is disadvantaged with respect to a dominant group in terms of social status, education, employment, wealth and political power.
Anti-Defamation League	The Anti-Defamation League is an advocacy group founded in 1913 by B'nai B'rith in the United States whose stated aim is "to stop, by appeals to reason and conscience and, if necessary, by appeals to law, the defamation of the Jewish people. Its ultimate purpose is to secure justice and fair treatment to all citizens alike and to put an end forever to unjust and unfair discrimination against and ridicule of any sect or body of citizens."
Tolerance	Tolerance is a term used in social, cultural and religious contexts to describe attitudes and practices that prohibit discrimination against those practices or group memberships that may be disapproved of by those in the majority.
Homosexuality	Homosexuality can refer to both attraction or sexual behavior between people of the same sex, or to a sexual orientation. When describing the latter, it refers to enduring sexual and romantic attraction towards those of the same sex, but not necessarily to sexual behavior.
African Americans	African Americans are citizens or residents of the United States whose ancestors, usually in predominant part, were indigenous to Sub-Saharan Africa. Most are the descendants of captive Africans who were enslaved within the boundaries of the present United States.
Community	A community is a social group of organisms sharing an environment, normally with shared interests. In human communities, intent, belief, resources, preferences, needs, risks and a number of other conditions may be present and common, affecting the identity of the participants and their degree of

Chapter 1. Perspectives on Hate and Violence

Chapter 1. Perspectives on Hate and Violence

	cohesiveness.
Culture	Culture generally refers to patterns of human activity and the symbolic structures that give such activity significant importance. Culture has been called "the way of life for an entire society." As such, it includes codes of manners, dress, language, religion, rituals, norms of behavior such as law and morality, and systems of belief.
Justice	Justice concerns the proper ordering of things and persons within a society. As a concept it has been subject to philosophical, legal, and theological reflection and debate throughout history.
Latino	Latino is a term that is historically denoted relation to the ancient Latina tribe, who were an ancient Italic people who migrated to central Italy. Since its official adoption, the definition and usage of the term by the Federal Government is strictly as an ethnic, as opposed to racial, identifier, used together with the term Hispanic.
National Deviancy Conference	The National Deviancy Conference consisted of a group of British Criminologists dissatisfied with Orthodox British Criminology, many of them later involved with Critical criminology and/or Left realism.
White American	White American is an umbrella term officially employed by the United States Census Bureau, Office of Management and Budget and other U.S. government for the classification of American citizens or resident aliens "having origins in any of the original peoples of Europe,[5] the Middle East, or North Africa".[6] Included in the category are White Hispanics representing 7.73% of the total US population in 2006.[2]
American Nazi Party	The American Nazi Party is a group which formed on March 8, 1959 by George Lincoln Rockwell with the intent of reviving Nazism in the United States. The organization was based largely upon the ideals and policies of Adolf Hitler's NSDAP in Germany during the Third Reich along with the added platform of strong Holocaust denial.
Funding	Funding is to provide capital, which means money for a project, a person, a business or any other private or public institutions.
Gay	Gay usually describes a person's sexual orientation, being the standard term for homosexual. Gay sometimes also refers to commonalities shared by homosexual people, as in "gay history", the ideological concept of a hypothetical gay culture, as in "gay music." The word gay is sometimes used to refer to same-sex relationships.
Gender	Gender refers to the differences between men and women. Gender identity is an individual's self-conception as being male or female, as distinguished from actual biological sex. In general, gender often refers to purely social rather than biological differences.
Nonverbal communication	Nonverbal communication is usually understood as the process of sending and receiving wordless messages. Such messages can be communicated through gesture; body language or posture; facial expression and eye contact.
Sexuality	Generally speaking, sexuality is how people experience and express themselves as sexual beings. Sociologically, it can cover the cultural, political, and legal aspects; and philosophically, it can span the moral, ethical, theological, spiritual or religious aspects.
Communication	Communication is a process that allows organisms to exchange information by several methods. Communication requires that all parties understand a common language that is exchanged. There are auditory means, such as speaking, singing and sometimes tone of voice, and nonverbal, physical means, such as body language.
Lesbian	A lesbian is a woman who is romantically and sexually attracted only to other women. Some women in same-sex relationships do not identify as lesbian, but as bisexual, queer, or another label. As with any interpersonal activity, sexual expression depends on the context of the relationship.
Affirmative	Affirmative action refers to policies intended to promote access to education or employment aimed at

Chapter 1. Perspectives on Hate and Violence

action	a historically socio-politically non-dominant group. Motivation for affirmative action policies is to redress the effects of past discrimination and to encourage public institutions such as universities, hospitals and police forces to be more representative of the population.
Hitler, Adolph	Hitler, Adolph as the leader of the National Socialist German Workers Party. He was appointed Chancellor of Germany and became leader remaining in power until his suicide. After restructuring the economy and rearming the military, a dictatorship commonly characterized as totalitarian or fascist was established. He pursued an aggressive foreign policy, with an ideological goal of Lebensraum.
Holocaust	The Holocaust is the term generally used to describe the killing of approximately six million European Jews during World War II, as part of a program of deliberate extermination planned and executed by the National Socialist regime in Germany led by Adolf Hitler.
Nazism	Nazism, a form of National Socialism, refers primarily to the totalitarian ideology and practices of the Nazi Party under Adolf Hitler. It also refers to the policies adopted by the government of Germany, a period in German history known as Nazi Germany or the "Third Reich".
Political party	A political party is a political organization that seeks to attain political power within a government, usually by participating in electoral campaigns. Parties often espouse a certain ideology and vision, but may also represent a coalition among disparate interests.
Denial	Denial is a defense mechanism in which a person is faced with a fact that is too uncomfortable to accept and rejects it instead, insisting that it is not true despite what may be overwhelming evidence.
National Crime Victimization Survey	The National Crime Victimization Survey, administered by the Bureau of Justice Statistics, is a national survey of approximately 42,000 households in the United States, on the frequency of crime victimization, as well as chacteristics and consequences of victimization.
Victimology	Victimology is the study of why certain people are victims of crime and how lifestyles affect the chances that a certain person will fall victim to a crime. The field can cover a wide number of disciplines, including sociology, psychology, criminal justice, law and advocacy.
Catholics	The number of Catholics in the world is around 1.1 billion and continues to increase, particularly in Africa and Asia. Brazil is the country with the largest number of Catholics. Catholics believe that God works actively in the world. Catholics grow in grace through participation in the sacramental life of the Church, and through prayer, the work of mercy, and spiritual disciplines such as fasting and pilgrimage.
Islam	Islam is a monotheistic religion originating with the teachings of Muhammad, a 7th-century Arab religious and political figure. Islam includes many religious practices. Adherents are generally required to observe the Five Pillars of Islam, which are five duties that unite Muslims into a community.
Timothy McVeigh	Timothy McVeigh was a decorated United States Army veteran and security guard who bombed the Alfred P. Murrah Federal Building in Oklahoma City. He was convicted of eleven United States federal offenses, and was sentenced to death and executed for his role. He claimed that the bombing was revenge for "what the U.S. government did at Waco and Ruby Ridge."
Muslim	A Muslim is an adherent of the religion of Islam. They believe that there is only one God, translated in Arabic as Allah. They also believe that Islam existed long before Muhammad and that the religion has evolved with time.
Oklahoma City bombing	The Oklahoma City bombing was an attack on April 19, 1995 aimed at the Alfred P. Murrah Federal Building, a U.S. government office complex in downtown Oklahoma City, Oklahoma. The attack claimed 168 lives and left over 800 injured. Until the September 11, 2001 attacks, it was the deadliest act of terrorism on U.S. soil.

Go to **Cram101.com** for the Practice Tests for this Chapter.

Chapter 1. Perspectives on Hate and Violence

Chapter 1. Perspectives on Hate and Violence

Iraq war	The Iraq War is an ongoing conflict with the United States-led invasion of Iraq. The main rationale for the Iraq War offered by U.S. President George W. Bush, former Prime Minister of the United Kingdom Tony Blair, former Prime Minister of Spain José María Aznar and their domestic and foreign supporters, was the belief that Iraq possessed and was actively developing weapons of mass destruction.
Balbir Singh Sodhi	Balbir Singh Sodhi was a Mesa, Arizona, gas station owner who was murdered in the aftermath of the September 11, 2001 attacks. He made headlines because he was the first of several cases across the United States that were reported to the police as acts of retaliation for the terrorist attacks. According to family members, Singh Sodhi had been distraught because of the terrorist attacks.
Perception	Perception is the process of attaining awareness or understanding of sensory information.
Terrorism	Terrorism is a term used to describe violence or other harmful acts committed (or threatened) against civilians by groups or persons for political, nationalist, or religious goals. As a type of unconventional warfare, terrorism means to weaken or supplant existing political landscapes through capitulation, acquiescence, or radicalization, as opposed to subversion or direct military action.
Intifada	Intifada is an Arabic word for shaking off, though it is generally translated into English as rebellion.
Nativism	Although opposition to immigration is a feature of all countries with immigration, the term nativism originated in American politics and has a specific meaning. Strictly speaking, the term nativism distinguishes between Americans who were born in the United States, and individuals who have immigrated - 'first generation' immigrants.
Anti-Semitism	Anti-semitism is hostility toward or prejudice against Jews as a religious, racial, or ethnic group, which can range in expression from individual hatred to institutionalized, violent persecution.
Al Gore	Al Gore is an American environmental activist, author, businessperson, and former politician.
Tom Metzger	Tom Metzger is the founder of the White Aryan Resistance. Metzger has been incarcerated in Los Angeles County, California and Toronto, Ontario, and has been involved in several government inquiries and lawsuits. He has participated in race discussions and interviews with CNN and Telemundo, and has appeared in numerous documentaries about White nationalism.
National Association for the Advancement of Colored People	The National Association for the Advancement of Colored People is one of the oldest and most influential radical civil rights organizations in the United States. It was founded on February 12, 1909 by a diverse group composed of W.E.B. Du Bois, Ida Wells-Barnett, Henry Moskowitz, Mary White Ovington, Oswald Garrison Villard, and William English Walling, to work on behalf of the rights of African Americans. Its name, retained in accord with tradition, is one of the last surviving uses of the term "colored people." The group is based in Baltimore, Maryland.
Resistance	Psychological resistance is the phenomenon often encountered in clinical practice in which patients either directly or indirectly oppose changing their behavior or refuse to discuss, remember, or think about presumably clinically relevant experiences.
White Aryan Resistance	The White Aryan Resistance is a neo-Nazi white supremacist organization founded and led by former Ku Klux Klan leader Tom Metzger. It holds views which are self-described as racist, as seen in their website sections "Racist Jokes" and "Racist Videos," and in the tagline for their newspaper The Insurgent, as "the most racist newspaper on earth."
Louis Farrakhan	Louis Farrakhan is the Supreme Minister of the Nation of Islam as the National Representative of Elijah Muhammad. He is also well-known as an advocate for African American interests and a critic of American society. Farrakhan currently resides in Kenwood, an affluent neighborhood on the south side of Chicago, and part time at a Nation of Islam farm in New Buffalo, Michigan.
Partnership	A partnership is a type of business entity in which partners share with each other the profits or losses of the business undertaking in which all have invested.

Chapter 1. Perspectives on Hate and Violence

Drug	A drug is any chemical or biological substance, synthetic or non-synthetic, that when taken into the organism's body, will in some way alter the functions of that organism. This broad definition can be taken to include such substances as food.
Ruby Ridge	Ruby Ridge was a fire-fight and stand-off between white separatist Randy Weaver, his family and associates, and agents of the U.S. Marshals and the FBI in August of 1992.
Violent crime	A violent crime or crime of violence is a crime in which the offender uses or threatens to use violent force upon the victim. The United States Department of Justice Bureau of Justice Statistics (BJS) counts five categories of crime as violent crimes: murder, rape, robbery, aggravated assault, and simple assault.
Conspiracy	In the criminal law, a conspiracy is an agreement between natural persons to break the law at some time in the future, and, in some cases, with at least one overt act in furtherance of that agreement. There is no limit on the number participating in the conspiracy and, in most countries, no requirement that any steps have been taken to put the plan into effect compare attempts which require proximity to the full offence.
Coming into force	Coming into force refers to the date and process by which legislation, or part of legislation, comes to have legal force and effect.
Law enforcement	Law Enforcement is a term used to describe either an organization that enforces the laws of one or more governing bodies, or an organisation that actively and directly assists in the enforcement of laws.
Military	Military has two broad meanings. In its first sense, it refers to soldiers and soldiering. In its second sense, it refers to armed forces as a whole.
American Dilemma	An American Dilemma: The Negro Problem and Modern Democracy is a 1944 study of race relations authored by Swedish economist Gunnar Myrdal and funded by The Carnegie Foundation. The foundation chose Myrdal because it thought that as a non-American, he could offer a more unbiased opinion. Myrdal's volume, at nearly 1,500 pages, painstakingly detailed what he saw as obstacles to full participation in American society that were faced by African-Americans as of the 1940s. It sold over 100,000 copies and went through 25 printings before going into its second edition in 1965. It was enormously influential in how racial issues were viewed in the United States, and it was cited in the landmark Brown v. Board case "in general." The book was generally positive in its outlook on the future of race relations in America, taking the view that democracy would triumph over racism. In many ways it laid the groundwork for future policies of racial integration and affirmative action.
An American Dilemma	An American Dilemma: The Negro Problem and Modern Democracy is a 1944 study of race relations authored by Swedish economist Gunnar Myrdal and funded by The Carnegie Foundation.
Culture of poverty	The culture of poverty concept is a social theory explaining the cycle of poverty. Based on the concept that the poor have a unique value system, the culture of poverty theory suggests the poor remain in poverty because of their adaptations to the burdens of poverty.
Poverty	Poverty may be seen as the collective condition of poor people, or of poor groups, and in this sense entire nation-states are sometimes regarded as poor. Although the most severe poverty is in the developing world, there is evidence of poverty in every region.
Moynihan Report	The Moynihan Report hypothesized that the destruction of the Black nuclear-family structure would hinder further progress towards economic, and thus political, equality. The report concluded that the structure of family life in the black community constituted a 'tangle of pathology...capable of perpetuating itself without assistance from the white world,' and that 'at the heart of the deterioration of the fabric of Negro society is the deterioration of the Negro family.
Daniel Patrick Moynihan	Daniel Patrick Moynihan was an American politician and sociologist. He was an Assistant Secretary of Labor for policy in the Kennedy Administration and in the early part of the Lyndon Johnson Administration. He coined the term "professionalization of reform" by which the government

Chapter 1. Perspectives on Hate and Violence

Chapter 1. Perspectives on Hate and Violence

	bureaucracy thinks up problems for government to solve rather than simply responding to problems identified elsewhere.
Anti-intellectualism	Anti-intellectualism describes a sentiment of hostility towards, or mistrust of, intellectuals and intellectual pursuits.
Cult	In religion and sociology, a cult is a cohesive group of people devoted to beliefs or practices that the surrounding culture or society considers to be far outside the mainstream, sometimes reaching the point of a taboo.
Intelligence	Intelligence is a property of mind that encompasses many related abilities, such as the capacities to reason, to plan, to solve problems, to think abstractly, to comprehend ideas, to use language, and to learn. In some cases, intelligence may include traits such as: creativity, personality, character, knowledge, or wisdom.
Bell Curve	The Bell Curve is a controversial, best-selling book by the late Harvard professor Richard J. Herrnstein and American Enterprise Institute political pundit Charles Murray. Its central point is that intelligence is a better predictor of many factors including financial income, job performance, unwed pregnancy, and crime than parent's Socio-Economic status or education level.
Richard Herrnstein	Richard Herrnstein was a prominent researcher in animal learning in the Skinnerian tradition. He was one of the founders of Quantitative Analysis of Behavior. His major research finding as an experimental psychologist is called "Matching law" -- the tendency of animals to allocate their choices in direct proportion to the rewards they provide.
Meritocracy	A social system in which status is assumed to be acquired through individual ability and effort is referred to as a meritocracy.
Homicide	Homicide refers to the act of killing another human being. It can also describe a person who has committed such an act, though this use is rare in modern English. Although homicide does not define an illegal act necessarily, sometimes it is used synonymously with "murder."
Crow	The Crow are a tribe of Native Americans who historically lived in the Yellowstone River valley and now live on a reservation south of Billings, Montana. Traditional clothing the Crow wore depended on gender. Women tended to wear simple clothes. Male clothing usually consisted of a shirt, trimmed leggings with a belt, a robe, and moccasins. Women held a very significant role within the tribe.
De facto	De facto is a Latin expression that means "in fact" or "in practice" but not spelled out by law. The term de facto may also be used when there is no relevant law or standard, but a common practice is well established, although perhaps not quite universal. A de facto standard is a technical or other standard that is so dominant that everybody seems to follow it like an authorized standard.
De facto segregation	Segregation that is an unintended consequence of social or ecological arrangements is referred to as de facto segregation.
Jim Crow laws	The Jim Crow Laws were state and local laws enacted in the Southern and border states of the United States. They mandated "separate but equal" status for black Americans. In reality, this led to treatment and accommodations that were almost always inferior to those provided to white Americans.
Segregation	Segregation may be mandated by law or exist through social norms. Segregation may be maintained by means ranging from discrimination in hiring and in the rental and sale of housing to certain races to vigilante violence such as lynchings; a situation that arises when members of different races mutually prefer to associate and do business with members of their own race would usually be described as separation or de facto separation of the races rather than segregation.

Chapter 1. Perspectives on Hate and Violence

Chapter 2. A Typology of Hate

Interest group	An interest group is an organized collection of people who seek to influence political decisions.
Anti-Defamation League	The Anti-Defamation League is an advocacy group founded in 1913 by B'nai B'rith in the United States whose stated aim is "to stop, by appeals to reason and conscience and, if necessary, by appeals to law, the defamation of the Jewish people. Its ultimate purpose is to
Crime	A normative definition views crime as deviant behavior that violates prevailing norms, specifically, cultural standards prescribing how humans ought to behave.
Federal Bureau of Investigation	The Federal Bureau of Investigation is the primary investigative arm of the United States Department of Justice, serving as both a federal criminal investigative body and a domestic intelligence agency.
Poverty	Poverty may be seen as the collective condition of poor people, or of poor groups, and in this sense entire nation-states are sometimes regarded as poor. Although the most severe poverty is in the developing world, there is evidence of poverty in every region.
Southern Poverty Law Center	The Southern Poverty Law Center is an American non-profit legal organization, internationally known for its tolerance education programs, its legal victories against white supremacists and its tracking of hate groups.
Uniform Crime Reports	The Uniform Crime Reports are crime indexes, published annually by the Federal Bureau of Investigation (FBI). The reports summarize the incidence and rate of reported crimes within the United States.
Cooperation	Cooperation is the practice of individuals or larger societal entities working in common with mutually agreed-upon goals and possibly methods, instead of working separately in competition, and in which the success of one is dependent and contingent upon the success of another.
Groups	In sociology, a group can be defined as two or more humans that interact with one another, accept expectations and obligations as members of the group, and share a common identity. By this definition, society can be viewed as a large group, though most social groups are considerably smaller.
Hatred	Hatred is an emotion of intense revulsion, distaste, enmity, or antipathy for a person, thing, or phenomenon, generally attributed to a desire to avoid, restrict, remove, or destroy the hated object. Hatred can be based on fear of an object or past negative consequences of dealing with that object.
Police	Police are agents or agencies empowered to effect public and social order through various means of coercion including the legitimate use of force.
James Byrd, Jr.	James Byrd, Jr. was an African-American murdered in 1998 by Shawn Allen Berry, Lawrence Russell Brewer, and John William King, in Jasper, Texas.
Disability	Disability is lack of ability relative to a personal or group standard or spectrum. Disability may involve physical impairment, sensory impairment, cognitive or intellectual impairment, mental disorder also known as psychiatric disability, or various types of chronic disease. A disability may occur during a person's lifetime or may be present from birth.
Hate crimes	Hate crimes occur when a perpetrator targets a victim because of his or her membership in a certain social group, usually defined by race, religion, sexual orientation, disability, ethnicity, nationality, age, gender, gender identity, or political affiliation. Hate crimes differ from conventional crime because they are not directed simply at an individual, but are meant to cause fear and intimidation in an entire group or class of people.
Homosexuality	Homosexuality can refer to both attraction or sexual behavior between people of the same sex, or to a sexual orientation. When describing the latter, it refers to enduring sexual and

Chapter 2. A Typology of Hate

Chapter 2. A Typology of Hate

	romantic attraction towards those of the same sex, but not necessarily to sexual behavior.
Ku Klux Klan	Ku Klux Klan is the name of several past and present organizations in the United States that have advocated white supremacy, antisemitism, racism, homophobia, and nativism. These organizations have often used terrorism, violence and acts of intimidation, such as cross lighting to oppress African Americans, and other social or ethnic groups.
Race	The term race refers to the concept of dividing people into populations or groups on the basis of various sets of characteristics and beliefs about common ancestry. The most widely used human racial categories are based on visible traits especially skin color, facial features and hair texture, and self-identification.
Sadism	Sadism refers to sexual or non-sexual gratification in the infliction of pain or humiliation upon or by another person.
Sexuality	Generally speaking, sexuality is how people experience and express themselves as sexual beings. Sociologically, it can cover the cultural, political, and legal aspects; and philosophically, it can span the moral, ethical, theological, spiritual or religious aspects.
Victimology	Victimology is the study of why certain people are victims of crime and how lifestyles affect the chances that a certain person will fall victim to a crime. The field can cover a wide number of disciplines, including sociology, psychology, criminal justice, law and advocacy.
Aryan	Aryan is an English language word derived from Sanskrit and Avestan ârya- meaning "noble". It is widely held to have been used as an ethnic self-designation of the Proto-Indo-Iranians. Since, in the 19th century, the Indo-Iranians were the most ancient known speakers of Indo-European languages, the word Aryan was adopted to refer not only to the Indo-Iranian people, but also to Indo-European speakers as a whole.
Aryan Nation	The Aryan Nation is a White Nationalist, Neo-Nazi organization which was founded by Richard Girnt Butler as an arm of the Christian Identity group Church of Jesus Christ-Christian. The group has been called a "terrorist threat" by the FBI, and the RAND Corporation has called it the "first truly nationwide terrorist network." Its origin lies in the teachings of Wesley Swift, a significant figure in the early Christian Identity movement.
Aryan Nations	Aryan Nations is an international white supremacist, Neo-Nazi organization. It was founded in the 1970s by Richard Girnt Butler as an arm of the Christian Identity group Church of Jesus Christ-Christian.
Resistance	Psychological resistance is the phenomenon often encountered in clinical practice in which patients either directly or indirectly oppose changing their behavior or refuse to discuss, remember, or think about presumably clinically relevant experiences.
Social psychology	Social psychology refers to the study of the effects of social environments on the psychological functioning of individuals.
White Aryan Resistance	The White Aryan Resistance is a neo-Nazi white supremacist organization founded and led by former Ku Klux Klan leader Tom Metzger. It holds views which are self-described as racist, as seen in their website sections "Racist Jokes" and "Racist Videos," and in the tagline for their newspaper The Insurgent, as "the most racist newspaper on earth."
Psychology	Psychology is both an academic and applied discipline involving the scientific study of mental processes and behavior. Psychology is one of the behavioral sciences a broad field that spans the social and natural sciences. It attempts to understand the role human behavior plays in social dynamics while incorporating physiological and neurological processes into its conceptions of mental functioning.
American Nazi Party	The American Nazi Party is a group which formed on March 8, 1959 by George Lincoln Rockwell with the intent of reviving Nazism in the United States. The organization was based largely

Go to **Cram101.com** for the Practice Tests for this Chapter.

Chapter 2. A Typology of Hate

Chapter 2. A Typology of Hate

	upon the ideals and policies of Adolf Hitler's NSDAP in Germany during the Third Reich along with the added platform of strong Holocaust denial.
Identity	Identity is an umbrella term used throughout the social sciences to describe an individual's comprehension of him or herself as a discrete, separate entity.
Ukraine	Ukraine ranked 28th in the world and estimated at $355.8 billions. Nominal GDP was $81.53 billions, ranked 53rd in the world. In Soviet times, the economy of the republic was the second largest in the Soviet Union, being an important industrial and agricultural component of the country's planned economy. With the collapse of the Soviet system, the country moved from a planned economy to a market economy. The transition process was painful for the majority of the population which plunged into poverty.
Militia	A Militia is an organization of citizens to provide defense, emergency or paramilitary service, or those engaged in such activity.
Oklahoma City bombing	The Oklahoma City bombing was an attack on April 19, 1995 aimed at the Alfred P. Murrah Federal Building, a U.S. government office complex in downtown Oklahoma City, Oklahoma. The attack claimed 168 lives and left over 800 injured. Until the September 11, 2001 attacks, it was the deadliest act of terrorism on U.S. soil.
White supremacy	White supremacy is a racist paradigm based on the assertion that white people are superior to other races. The term is sometimes used specifically to describe a political ideology that advocates social and political dominance for whites.
Government	A government is a body that has the authority to make and the power to enforce laws within a civil, corporate, religious, academic, or other organization or group.
Ruby Ridge	Ruby Ridge was a fire-fight and stand-off between white separatist Randy Weaver, his family and associates, and agents of the U.S. Marshals and the FBI in August of 1992.
Creativity Movement	The Creativity Movement is an often violent United States-based white supremacist organization that advocates a whites-only religion called Creativity. The movement's use of the term creator does not refer to a deity, but rather to themselves.
First Amendment	The First Amendment to the United States Constitution is a part of the United States Bill of Rights that expressly prohibits the United States Congress from making laws "respecting an establishment of religion" or that prohibit free exercise of religion, laws that infringe the freedom of speech, infringe the freedom of the press, limit the right to peaceably assemble, or limit the right to petition the government for a redress of grievances.
Bigotry	A bigot is a person who is intolerant of opinions, lifestyles, or identities differing from his or her own, and bigotry is the corresponding state of mind. Forms of bigotry may have a related ideology or world views.
Lifestyle	In sociology a lifestyle is the way a person lives. This includes patterns of social relations, consumption, entertainment, and dress. A lifestyle typically also reflects an individual's attitudes, values or worldview.
Murder	Murder is the unlawful, premeditated killing of a human being by another. The penalty for murder is usually either life imprisonment, or in jurisdictions with capital punishment, the death penalty.
Music	Music is an art form in which the medium is sound organized in time. Common elements of music are pitch, rhythm, dynamics, and the sonic qualities of timbre and texture. The word derives from Greek μουσική, " of the Muses".
Nativism	Although opposition to immigration is a feature of all countries with immigration, the term nativism originated in American politics and has a specific meaning. Strictly speaking, the term nativism distinguishes between Americans who were born in the United States, and

Chapter 2. A Typology of Hate

Chapter 2. A Typology of Hate

	individuals who have immigrated - 'first generation' immigrants.
Anti-semitism	Anti-semitism is hostility toward or prejudice against Jews as a religious, racial, or ethnic group, which can range in expression from individual hatred to institutionalized, violent persecution.
African Americans	African Americans are citizens or residents of the United States whose ancestors, usually in predominant part, were indigenous to Sub-Saharan Africa. Most are the descendants of captive Africans who were enslaved within the boundaries of the present United States.
Columbine High School	Columbine High School is a secondary school in unincorporated Jefferson County, Colorado. Columbine High School was the site of the fourth deadliest school massacre in modern United States history, which took place April 20, 1999.
Columbine High School massacre	The Columbine High School massacre occurred on Tuesday, April 20, 1999, at Columbine High School in Columbine in unincorporated Jefferson County, Colorado, near Denver and Littleton. Two students, Eric Harris and Dylan Klebold, embarked on a shooting rampage, killing 12 students and a teacher, as well as wounding 23 others, before committing suicide.
Eric Harris and Dylan Klebold	Eric Harris and Dylan Klebold were the high school seniors who committed the Columbine High School massacre. They killed 13 people and injured 24 others. Both Harris, 18 years old, and Klebold, 17, committed suicide after the killings.
Migration	The movement of people from one country or region to another in order to settle permanently, is referred to as a migration.
Minority	A minority is a sociological group that does not constitute a politically dominant plurality of the total population of a given society. A sociological minority is not necessarily a numerical minority it may include any group that is disadvantaged with respect to a dominant group in terms of social status, education, employment, wealth and political power.
Neighborhood	A neighborhood is a geographically localized community located within a larger city, town or suburb. Traditionally, a neighborhood is small enough that the neighbors are all able to know each other.
Cross burning	Cross burning is a practice widely associated with the Ku Klux Klan as a reminder of faith. In the early 20th century, the Klan burnt Christian crosses on hillsides or near the homes of those they wished to intimidate, usually non-Caucasians.
Racism	Racism, by its simplest definition, is discrimination based on race. People with racist beliefs might hate certain groups of people according to their race, or in the case of institutional racism, certain racial groups may be denied rights or benefits. Racism typically starts with the assumption that there are taxonomic differences between different groups of people. According to the United Nations conventions, there is no distinction between the term racial discrimination and ethnic discrimination.
Prejudice	Prejudice is, as the name implies, the process of "pre-judging" something. It implies coming to a judgment on a subject before learning where the preponderance of evidence actually lies, or forming a judgment without direct experience.
Symbolism	The term symbolism is often limited to use in contrast to "representationalism"; defining the general directions of a linear spectrum - where in all symbolic concepts can be viewed in relation, and where changes in context may imply systemic changes to individual and collective definitions of symbols. "Symbolism" may refer to a way of choosing representative symbols in line with abstract rather than literal properties, allowing for the broader interpretation of a carried meaning than more literal concept-representations allow.
Economics	Economics is the social science that studies the production, distribution, and consumption of goods and services. One of the uses of economics is to explain how economies work and what

Chapter 2. A Typology of Hate

Chapter 2. A Typology of Hate

	the relations are between economic players in the larger society.
Japanese American Citizens League	The Japanese American Citizens League was formed in 1929 to protect the rights of Japanese Americans from the state and federal governments. It fought for civil rights for Japanese Americans, assisted those in internment camps during World War II, and led a successful campaign for redress for internment from the U.S. Congress.
Terrorism	Terrorism is a term used to describe violence or other harmful acts committed (or threatened) against civilians by groups or persons for political, nationalist, or religious goals. As a type of unconventional warfare, terrorism means to weaken or supplant existing political landscapes through capitulation, acquiescence, or radicalization, as opposed to subversion or direct military action.
Timothy McVeigh	Timothy McVeigh was a decorated United States Army veteran and security guard who bombed the Alfred P. Murrah Federal Building in Oklahoma City. He was convicted of eleven United States federal offenses, and was sentenced to death and executed for his role. He claimed that the bombing was revenge for "what the U.S. government did at Waco and Ruby Ridge."
Texaco	Texaco is the name of an American oil retail brand.
War Crime	In the context of war, a war crime is a punishable offense under International Law, for violations of the laws of war by any person or persons, military or civilian.
Asian people	Asian people is a demonym for people from Asia. However, the use of the term varies by country and person, often referring to people from a particular region or subregion of Asia. Though it may be based on residence, it is also often considered a "racial group" or an ethnic group.
Nazism	Nazism, a form of National Socialism, refers primarily to the totalitarian ideology and practices of the Nazi Party under Adolf Hitler. It also refers to the policies adopted by the government of Germany, a period in German history known as Nazi Germany or the "Third Reich".
Generation	Generation is the act of producing offspring. It can also refer to the act of creating something inanimate such as electrical generation or cryptographic code generation.
Generations	Generations is the act of producing offspring. It can also refer to the act of creating something inanimate such as electrical generation or cryptographic code generation.
Inferiority	An inferiority complex, in the fields of psychology and psychoanalysis, is a feeling that one is inferior to others in some way. Such feelings can arise from an imagined or actual inferiority in the afflicted person. It is often subconscious, and is thought to drive afflicted individuals to overcompensate, resulting either in spectacular achievement or extreme antisocial behavior, or both. Unlike a normal feeling of inferiority, which can act as an incentive for achievement, an inferiority complex is an advanced state of discouragement, often resulting in a retreat from difficulties.
Apathy	Apathy is a psychological term for a state of indifference — where an individual is unresponsive or "indifferent" to aspects of emotional, social, or physical life. Clinical apathy is considered to be at an elevated level, while a moderate level might be considered depression, and an extreme level could be diagnosed as a dissociative disorder. The physical aspect of apathy associated with physical deterioration, muscle loss, and lack of energy is called lethargy — which has many pathological causes as well.
Europe	Europe is one of the traditional seven political continents, and a peninsular sub-continent of the geographic continent Eurasia. Europe is bounded to the north by the Arctic Ocean, to the west by the Atlantic Ocean, to the south by the Mediterranean Sea, and to the southeast by the Caucasus Mountains, the Black Sea and the waterways connecting the Black Sea to the Mediterranean. To the east, Europe is generally divided from Asia by the water divide of the Ural Mountains, the Ural River, and by the Caspian Sea.

Chapter 2. A Typology of Hate

Regime	A regime is the set of rules, both formal and informal that regulate the operation of government and its interactions with the economy and society.

Chapter 2. A Typology of Hate

Chapter 3. The Benefits of Bigotry

Protest	Protest expresses relatively overt reaction to events or situations: sometimes in favor, though more often opposed. Protesters may organize a protest as a way of publicly and forcefully making their opinions heard in an attempt to influence public opinion or
Anti-Semitism	Anti-semitism is hostility toward or prejudice against Jews as a religious, racial, or ethnic group, which can range in expression from individual hatred to institutionalized, violent persecution.
Honesty	Honesty is the human quality of communicating and acting truthfully related to truth as a value. This includes listening, and any action in the human repertoire as well as speaking. Quality of honesty applies to all behaviors. One cannot refuse to consider factual information.
Media	In communication, media are the storage and transmission tools used to store and deliver information or data. It is often referred to as synonymous with mass media or news media, but may refer to a single medium used to communicate any data for any purpose.
Ethics	Ethics, a major branch of philosophy, is the study of values and customs of a person or group. It covers the analysis and employment of concepts such as right and wrong, good and evil, and responsibility. It is divided into three primary areas: meta-ethics, normative ethics, and applied ethics.
Self-esteem	In psychology, self-esteem reflects a person's overall self-appraisal of his or her own worth.
Bigotry	A bigot is a person who is intolerant of opinions, lifestyles, or identities differing from his or her own, and bigotry is the corresponding state of mind. Forms of bigotry may have a related ideology or world views.
Authoritarianism	Authoritarianism describes a form of government characterized by strict obedience to the authority of the state, which often maintains and enforces social control through the use of oppressive measures. The term may also be used to describe the personality or management style of an individual or organization which seeks to dominate those within its sphere of influence and has little regard for building consensus.
Authoritarian Personality	A set of distinctive personality traits, including conformity, intolerance, and an inability to accept ambiguity, is referred to as an authoritarian personality.
Personality	In psychology, personality is a description of consistent emotional, thought, and behavior patterns in a person. The several theoretical perspectives on personality involve different ideas about the relationship between personality and other psychological constructs as well as different ideas about the way personality doesn't develop.
Ethnocentrism	Ethnocentrism is the tendency to look at the world primarily from the perspective of one's own culture. It often entails the belief that one's own race or ethnic group is the most important and/or that some or all aspects of its culture are superior to those of other groups.
Power	Power is the ability of a person to control or influence the choices of other persons. The term authority is often used for power perceived as legitimate by the social structure. Power can be seen as evil or unjust; indeed all evil and injustice committed by man against man involve power.
Dominance	In animal colonies, a condition established by one animal over another by prevailing in an aggressive encounter between the two, is referred to as dominance.
Columbine High School	Columbine High School is a secondary school in unincorporated Jefferson County, Colorado. Columbine High School was the site of the fourth deadliest school massacre in modern United States history, which took place April 20, 1999.

Chapter 3. The Benefits of Bigotry

Chapter 3. The Benefits of Bigotry

Columbine High School massacre	The Columbine High School massacre occurred on Tuesday, April 20, 1999, at Columbine High School in Columbine in unincorporated Jefferson County, Colorado, near Denver and Littleton. Two students, Eric Harris and Dylan Klebold, embarked on a shooting rampage, killing 12 students and a teacher, as well as wounding 23 others, before committing suicide.
Eric Harris and Dylan Klebold	Eric Harris and Dylan Klebold were the high school seniors who committed the Columbine High School massacre. They killed 13 people and injured 24 others. Both Harris, 18 years old, and Klebold, 17, committed suicide after the killings.
Mafia	The Mafia is an Italian criminal secret society. An offshoot emerged on the East Coast of the United States and in Australia following waves of Sicilian and Southern Italian emigration. In North America the Mafia often refers to Italian organized crime in general, rather than just traditional Sicilian organized crime.
Skinheads	Skinheads, named for their close-cropped or shaven heads, are a working-class subculture that originated in the United Kingdom in the late 1960s, and then spread to other parts of the world. The first skinheads were greatly influenced by West Indian rude boys and British mods, in terms of fashion, music and lifestyle. Originally, their subculture was primarily based on those elements, not politics or race. Since then, however, attitudes toward race and politics have become factors in where skinheads align themselves.
Bullying	Bullying is the act of intentionally causing harm to others through verbal harassment, physical assault, or other more subtle methods of coercion such as manipulation.
Washington	Washington is a state in the Pacific Northwest region of the United States. Named after George Washington, it is the only U.S. state named after a president.
Language	A language is a system of symbols and the rules used to manipulate them. Language can also refer to the use of such systems as a general phenomenon. Because a language also has a grammar, it can manipulate its symbols to express clear and regular relationships between them.
Hatred	Hatred is an emotion of intense revulsion, distaste, enmity, or antipathy for a person, thing, or phenomenon, generally attributed to a desire to avoid, restrict, remove, or destroy the hated object. Hatred can be based on fear of an object or past negative consequences of dealing with that object.
Labeling	Labeling is defining or describing a person in terms of his or her behavior. The term is often used in sociology to describe human interaction, control and identification of deviant behavior.
Minority	A minority is a sociological group that does not constitute a politically dominant plurality of the total population of a given society. A sociological minority is not necessarily a numerical minority it may include any group that is disadvantaged with respect to a dominant group in terms of social status, education, employment, wealth and political power.
American Indians	American Indians are the indigenous peoples from the regions of North America now encompassed by the continental United States, including parts of Alaska. They comprise a large number of distinct tribes, states, and ethnic groups, many of which survive as intact political communities. There has been a wide range of terms used to describe them and no consensus has been reached among indigenous members as to what they prefer.
Immigration	Although human migration has existed for hundreds of thousands of years, immigration in the modern sense refers to movement of people from one nation-state to another, where they are not citizens.
Religious persecution	Religious persecution is systematic mistreatment of an individual or group due to their religious affiliation.

Chapter 3. The Benefits of Bigotry

Chapter 3. The Benefits of Bigotry

Crow	The Crow are a tribe of Native Americans who historically lived in the Yellowstone River valley and now live on a reservation south of Billings, Montana. Traditional clothing the Crow wore depended on gender. Women tended to wear simple clothes. Male clothing usually consisted of a shirt, trimmed leggings with a belt, a robe, and moccasins. Women held a very significant role within the tribe.
Plessy v. Ferguson	Plessy v. Ferguson, 163 U.S. 537, was a landmark United States Supreme Court decision in the jurisprudence of the United States, upholding the constitutionality of racial segregation even in public accommodations, under the doctrine of "separate but equal".
Jim Crow laws	The Jim Crow Laws were state and local laws enacted in the Southern and border states of the United States. They mandated "separate but equal" status for black Americans. In reality, this led to treatment and accommodations that were almost always inferior to those provided to white Americans.
Segregation	Segregation may be mandated by law or exist through social norms. Segregation may be maintained by means ranging from discrimination in hiring and in the rental and sale of housing to certain races to vigilante violence such as lynchings; a situation that arises when members of different races mutually prefer to associate and do business with members of their own race would usually be described as separation or de facto separation of the races rather than segregation.
Mexican Americans	Mexican Americans are citizens of the United States of Mexican ancestry. Mexican Americans account for 9% of the country's population. Mexican Americans form the largest White Hispanic group in the United States. Mexican Americans trace their ancestry to Mexico and Mesoamerica, a country located in North America; the Southwest United States; bounded on the north by the United States; and many different European countries, especially Spain.
Stereotype	A stereotype is a simplified and/or standardized conception or image with specific meaning, often held in common by one group of people about another group. A stereotype can be a conventional and oversimplified conception, opinion, or image, based on the assumption that there are attributes that members of the other group hold in common. Stereotypes may be positive or negative in tone. They are typically generalizations based on minimal or limited knowledge about a group to which the person doing the stereotyping does not belong. Persons may be grouped based on race, ethnicity, religion, sexual orientation, or any number of other
Dawes Severalty Act	The Dawes Severalty Act authorized the President of the United States to have Native American tribal lands surveyed and divided into plots for individual Native American families. It was enacted on February 8, 1887 and named after its sponsor, U.S. Senator Henry L. Dawes of Massachusetts. The act was amended in 1891 and again in 1906 by the Burke Act. The act remained in effect until 1934.
Rodney King	Rodney King is an African-American taxi driver who became famous after his violent arrest by officers of the Los Angeles Police Department was videotaped by a bystander, George Holliday.
Los Angeles riots of 1992	The Los Angeles riots of 1992, also known as the Rodney King uprising or the Rodney King riots, were sparked on April 29, 1992 when a jury acquitted four police officers accused in the videotaped beating of black motorist Rodney King following a high-speed pursuit. Thousands of people in the Los Angeles area rioted over the six days following the verdict.
Police	Police are agents or agencies empowered to effect public and social order through various means of coercion including the legitimate use of force.
Cooperation	Cooperation is the practice of individuals or larger societal entities working in common with mutually agreed-upon goals and possibly methods, instead of working separately in competition, and in which the success of one is dependent and contingent upon the success of another.

Go to **Cram101.com** for the Practice Tests for this Chapter.

Chapter 3. The Benefits of Bigotry

Chapter 3. The Benefits of Bigotry

Race	The term race refers to the concept of dividing people into populations or groups on the basis of various sets of characteristics and beliefs about common ancestry. The most widely used human racial categories are based on visible traits especially skin color, facial features and hair texture, and self-identification.
Race riot	A race riot or racial riot is an outbreak of violent civil unrest in which race is a key factor.
Riot	Riot refers to a form of civil disorder characterized by disorganized groups lashing out in a sudden and intense rash of violence, vandalism or other crime. While a riot may be premeditated and intentionally incited, a true riot is quickly joined by people without foreknowledge of the riot.
Ethnic Group	An ethnic group is a population of human beings whose members identify with each other, usually on the basis of a presumed common genealogy or ancestry. Ethnicity is also defined from the recognition by others as a distinct group and by common cultural, linguistic, religious, behavioral or biological traits.
Groups	In sociology, a group can be defined as two or more humans that interact with one another, accept expectations and obligations as members of the group, and share a common identity. By this definition, society can be viewed as a large group, though most social groups are considerably smaller.
Victimology	Victimology is the study of why certain people are victims of crime and how lifestyles affect the chances that a certain person will fall victim to a crime. The field can cover a wide number of disciplines, including sociology, psychology, criminal justice, law and advocacy.
Political power	Political Power is a type of power held by a person or group in a society. There are many ways to hold such power. Officially, political power is held by the holders of sovereignty. Political power is not limited to head of states, however, and the extent to which a person or group holds such power is related to the amount of societal influence they can wield, formally or informally.
Muslim	A Muslim is an adherent of the religion of Islam. They believe that there is only one God, translated in Arabic as Allah. They also believe that Islam existed long before Muhammad and that the religion has evolved with time.

Go to **Cram101.com** for the Practice Tests for this Chapter.

Chapter 3. The Benefits of Bigotry

Chapter 4. The Production of Rebels, Deviants, and Other Decent People

Philip G. Zimbardo	Philip G. Zimbardo is an American psychologist and a professor emeritus at Stanford University. He is known for his Stanford prison experiment and his authorship of introductory psychology textbooks for college students.
Behavior	Behavior refers to the actions or reactions of an object or organism, usually in relation to the environment. Humans evaluate the acceptability of behavior using social norms and regulate behavior by means of social control. In sociology, behavior is considered as having no meaning, being not directed at other people and thus is the most basic human action.
Deviance	Deviance is behavior that is a recognized violation of social norms. Formal and informal social controls attempt to prevent or minimize it.
Armenian Genocide	The Armenian Genocide refers to the deliberate and systematic destruction of the Armenian population of the Ottoman Empire during and just after World War I. It was characterized by the use of massacres, and the use of deportations involving forced marches under conditions designed to lead to the death of the deportees, with the total number of Armenian deaths generally held to have been between one and one-and-a-half million.
Armenians	The Armenians are a nation and an ethnic group originating in the Caucasus and in the Armenian Highland. A large concentration of them has remained there, especially in Armenia, but many of them are also scattered elsewhere throughout the world. The Armenians have had a significant presence in countries such as Russia, Georgia and Iran due to their proximity to Armenia.
Turkey	Turkey is a Eurasian country that stretches across the Anatolian peninsula in western Asia and Thrace in the Balkan region of southeastern Europe. Turkey borders eight countries: Bulgaria to the northwest; Greece to the west, Georgia to the northeast; Armenia, Azerbaijan, and Iran to the east; and Iraq and Syria to the southeast.
Racism	Racism, by its simplest definition, is discrimination based on race. People with racist beliefs might hate certain groups of people according to their race, or in the case of institutional racism, certain racial groups may be denied rights or benefits. Racism typically starts with the assumption that there are taxonomic differences between different groups of people. According to the United Nations conventions, there is no distinction between the term racial discrimination and ethnic discrimination.
Competition	Competition is the act of striving against individuals or groups, for the purpose of achieving survival, income, pride, status, or other gain. It is a term that is commonly used in numerous fields, including business, economics, law, politics, ecology, music, and sports.
Contact	In Family Law, contact is one of the general terms which denotes the level of contact a parent or other significant person in a child's life can have with that child. Contact forms part of the bundle of rights and privileges which a parent may have in relation to any child of the family.
Desegregation	Desegregation is the process of ending racial segregation, most commonly used in reference to the United States. Desegregation was long a focus of the American Civil Rights Movement, both before and after the United States Supreme Court's decision in Brown v. Board of Education, particularly desegregation of the school systems and the military, as was the closely related but somewhat more ambitious goal of racial integration.
Hostility	Hostility is a form of angry internal rejection or denial in psychology.
Superordinate goals	Goals that both sides to a conflict seek and that tie their interests together rather than driving them apart are referred to as superordinate goals.
Groups	In sociology, a group can be defined as two or more humans that interact with one another, accept expectations and obligations as members of the group, and share a common identity. By this definition, society can be viewed as a large group, though most social groups are

Chapter 4. The Production of Rebels, Deviants, and Other Decent People

Chapter 4. The Production of Rebels, Deviants, and Other Decent People

	considerably smaller.
Hatred	Hatred is an emotion of intense revulsion, distaste, enmity, or antipathy for a person, thing, or phenomenon, generally attributed to a desire to avoid, restrict, remove, or destroy the hated object. Hatred can be based on fear of an object or past negative consequences of dealing with that object.
Thought	Thought is a mental form and process, respectively.
Ethnocentrism	Ethnocentrism is the tendency to look at the world primarily from the perspective of one's own culture. It often entails the belief that one's own race or ethnic group is the most important and/or that some or all aspects of its culture are superior to those of other groups.
Cooperation	Cooperation is the practice of individuals or larger societal entities working in common with mutually agreed-upon goals and possibly methods, instead of working separately in competition, and in which the success of one is dependent and contingent upon the success of another.
Military	Military has two broad meanings. In its first sense, it refers to soldiers and soldiering. In its second sense, it refers to armed forces as a whole.
Nazism	Nazism, a form of National Socialism, refers primarily to the totalitarian ideology and practices of the Nazi Party under Adolf Hitler. It also refers to the policies adopted by the government of Germany, a period in German history known as Nazi Germany or the "Third Reich".
Will	In common law, a will is a document by which a person regulates the rights of others over his or her property or family after death.
Freedom Riders	Civil Rights activists called Freedom Riders rode in interstate buses into the segregated southern United States to test the United States Supreme Court decision Boynton v. Virginia, 364 U.S. The first Freedom Ride left Washington D.C. on May 4, 1961, and was scheduled to arrive in New Orleans on May 17. Riders were arrested for trespassing, unlawful assembly, violating state and local Jim Crow laws, etc.
Leadership	Leadership is the ability to affect human behavior so as to accomplish a mission designated by the leader. Most research into leadership mistakenly focused on cognitive and intellectual processes, forgetting the important fact that every cognitive process is an embodied process.
Stanley Milgram	Stanley Milgram was a social psychologist at Yale University, Harvard University and the City University of New York. He conducted the Milgram experiment on obedience to authority. He also introduced the concept of familiar strangers.
New York	New York is a state in the Mid-Atlantic and Northeastern regions of the United States of America. With 62 counties, it is the country's third most populous state. It is bordered by Vermont, Massachusetts, Connecticut, New Jersey, and Pennsylvania, and shares a water border with Rhode Island as well as an international border with the Canadian provinces of Quebec and Ontario. Its five largest cities are New York City, Buffalo, Rochester, Yonkers, and Syracuse.
New York City	New York City two key demographic features are its population density and cultural diversity. It is exceptionally diverse. Throughout its history the city has been a major point of entry for immigrants; the term "melting pot" was first coined to describe densely populated immigrant neighborhoods on the Lower East Side. Violent crime in New York city has decreased 75% in the last twelve years and the murder rate.
Neighborhood	A neighborhood is a geographically localized community located within a larger city, town or suburb. Traditionally, a neighborhood is small enough that the neighbors are all able to know each other.

Go to **Cram101.com** for the Practice Tests for this Chapter.

Chapter 4. The Production of Rebels, Deviants, and Other Decent People

James Byrd, Jr.	James Byrd, Jr. was an African-American murdered in 1998 by Shawn Allen Berry, Lawrence Russell Brewer, and John William King, in Jasper, Texas.
Asch	Asch was a world-renowned American Gestalt psychologist and pioneer in social psychology. He became famous in the 1950s, following experiments which showed that social pressure can make a person say something that is obviously incorrect.
Solomon Asch	Solomon Asch was a world-renowned American Gestalt psychologist and pioneer in social psychology. He became famous following experiments which showed that social pressure can make a person say something that is obviously incorrect. He also cooperated with H. Witkin and inspired many ideas of the theory of cognitive style.
Community	A community is a social group of organisms sharing an environment, normally with shared interests. In human communities, intent, belief, resources, preferences, needs, risks and a number of other conditions may be present and common, affecting the identity of the participants and their degree of cohesiveness.
Minority	A minority is a sociological group that does not constitute a politically dominant plurality of the total population of a given society. A sociological minority is not necessarily a numerical minority it may include any group that is disadvantaged with respect to a dominant group in terms of social status, education, employment, wealth and political power.
Student	A student could be described as 'one who directs zeal at a subject'.
Violence	Violence is, on the one hand, acts of aggression and abuse that cause' or intend to cause injury to person or persons. Central to this concept of violence is the presence of the definite intention to cause significant injury, damage and harm.
Individualism	Individualism is a term used to describe a moral, political, or social outlook that stresses human independence and the importance of self-reliance and liberty. They promote the exercise of their goals and desires. They oppose most external interference with their choices - whether by society, the state, or any other group or institution.
Empathy	Empathy is commonly defined as one's ability to recognize, perceive and directly experientially feel the emotion of another. As the states of mind, beliefs, and desires of others are intertwined with their emotions, one with empathy for another may often be able to more effectively divine another's modes of thought and mood.
Victimology	Victimology is the study of why certain people are victims of crime and how lifestyles affect the chances that a certain person will fall victim to a crime. The field can cover a wide number of disciplines, including sociology, psychology, criminal justice, law and advocacy.
Compassion	Compassion is a profound and positive human emotion prompted by the pain of others.
Crime	A normative definition views crime as deviant behavior that violates prevailing norms, specifically, cultural standards prescribing how humans ought to behave.
Hate crimes	Hate crimes occur when a perpetrator targets a victim because of his or her membership in a certain social group, usually defined by race, religion, sexual orientation, disability, ethnicity, nationality, age, gender, gender identity, or political affiliation. Hate crimes differ from conventional crime because they are not directed simply at an individual, but are meant to cause fear and intimidation in an entire group or class of people.
Holocaust	The Holocaust is the term generally used to describe the killing of approximately six million European Jews during World War II, as part of a program of deliberate extermination planned and executed by the National Socialist regime in Germany led by Adolf Hitler.
Slavery	Slavery refers to an extreme form of stratification in which some people are owned by others.
Derrick Bell	Derrick Bell is a visiting professor of Constitutional Law at New York University School of

Chapter 4. The Production of Rebels, Deviants, and Other Decent People

Chapter 4. The Production of Rebels, Deviants, and Other Decent People

	Law for the past years and a major figure within the legal studies discipline of Critical Race Theory.
Columbine High School	Columbine High School is a secondary school in unincorporated Jefferson County, Colorado. Columbine High School was the site of the fourth deadliest school massacre in modern United States history, which took place April 20, 1999.
Columbine High School massacre	The Columbine High School massacre occurred on Tuesday, April 20, 1999, at Columbine High School in Columbine in unincorporated Jefferson County, Colorado, near Denver and Littleton. Two students, Eric Harris and Dylan Klebold, embarked on a shooting rampage, killing 12 students and a teacher, as well as wounding 23 others, before committing suicide.
Bigotry	A bigot is a person who is intolerant of opinions, lifestyles, or identities differing from his or her own, and bigotry is the corresponding state of mind. Forms of bigotry may have a related ideology or world views.
Gypsies	Gypsies is a term often considered derogatory for certain ethnic and cultural groups, and also inaccurately to refer to 'travellers' in general.
Refugee	According to the 1951 United Nations Convention Relating to the Status of a Refugee, a refugee is a person who owing to a well-founded fear of being persecuted for reasons of race, religion, nationality, membership of a particular social group, or political opinion, is outside the country of their nationality, and is unable to or, owing to such fear, is unwilling to avail him/herself of the protection of that country.
United Nations	The United Nations is an international organization whose stated aims are to facilitate cooperation in international law, international security, economic development, social progress and human rights issues.
United Nations High Commissioner for Refugees	United Nations High Commissioner for Refugees is a United Nations agency mandated to protect and support refugees at the request of a government or the UN itself and assists in their voluntary repatriation, local integration or resettlement to a third country.
Discrimination	Discrimination refers to the denial of equal access to social resources to people on the basis of their group membership.

Chapter 4. The Production of Rebels, Deviants, and Other Decent People